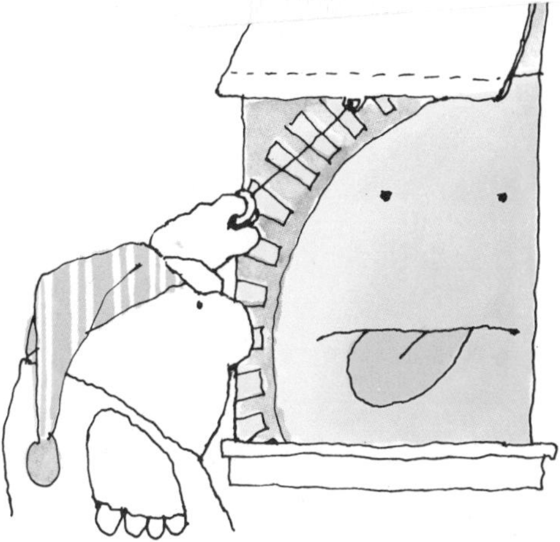

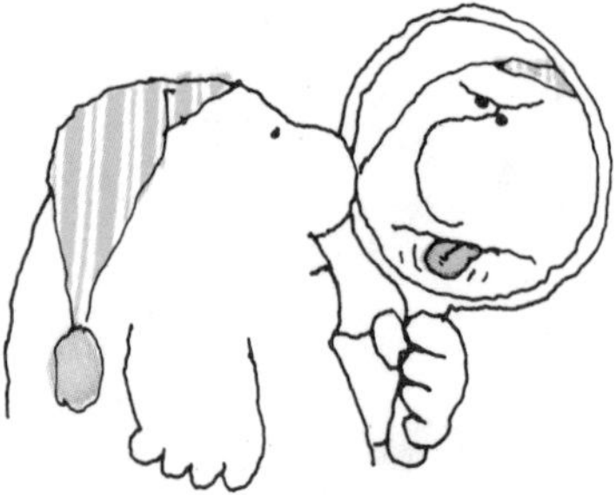

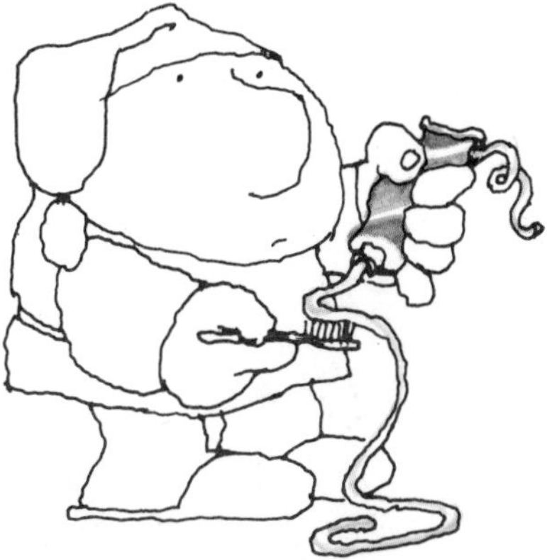

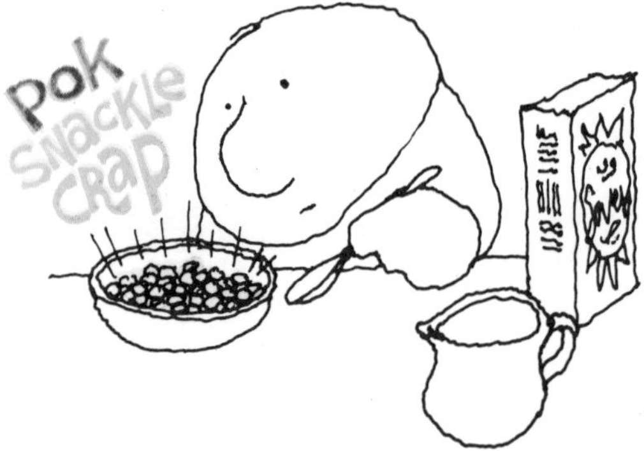
Pok
SNACKLE
CRAP

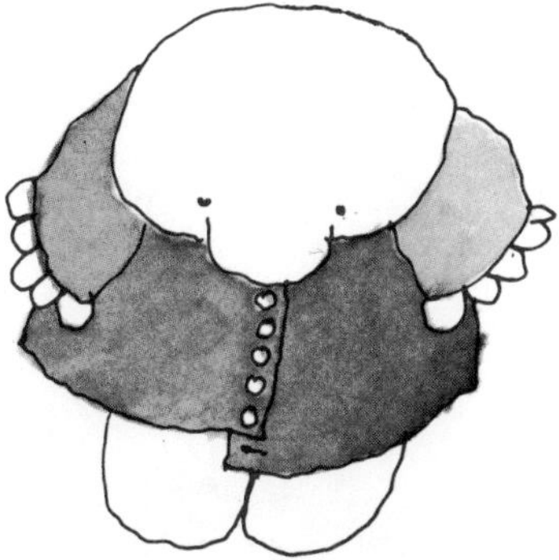

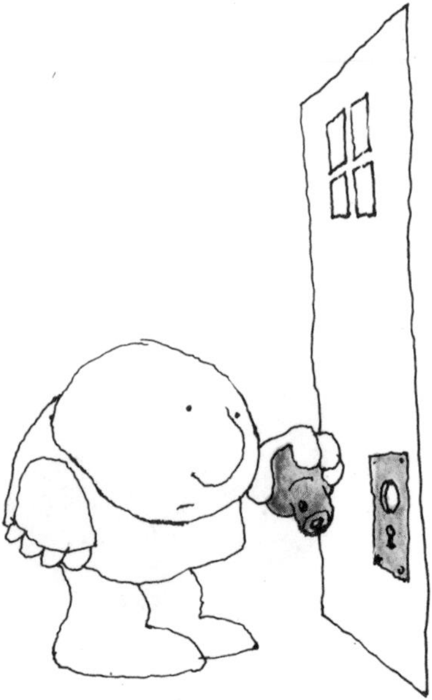

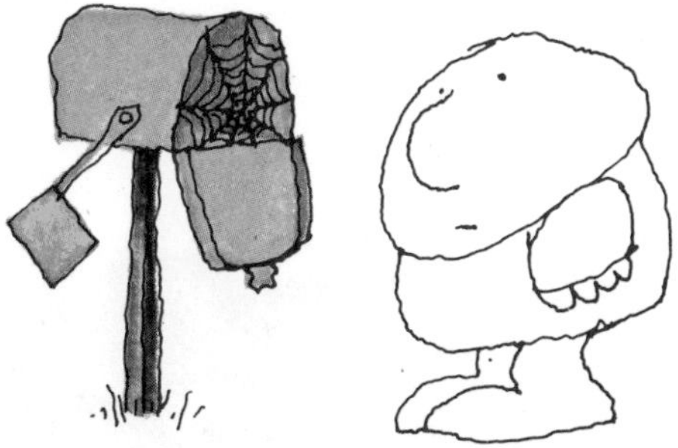

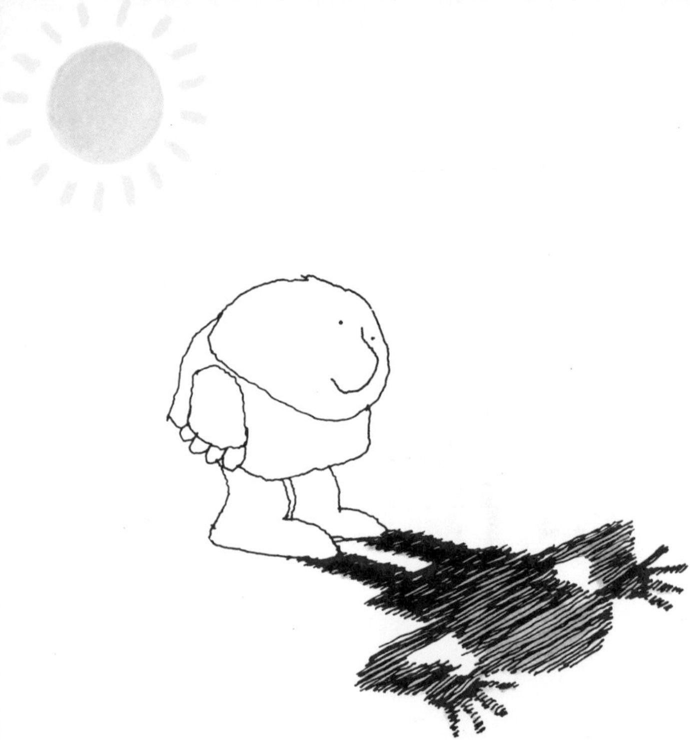

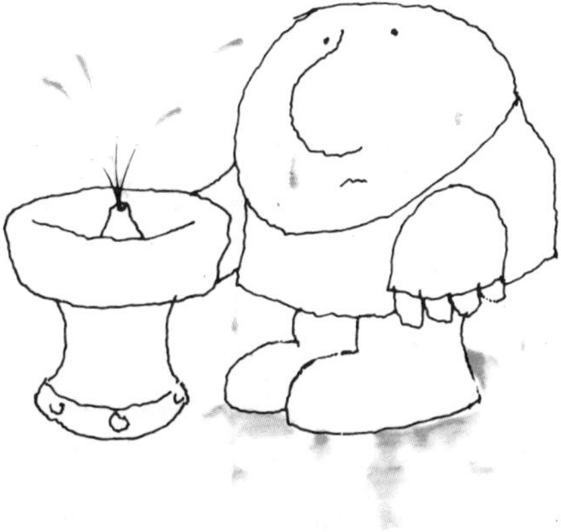

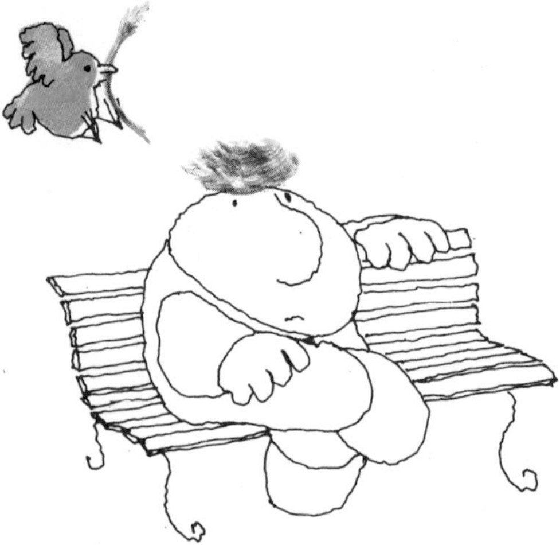

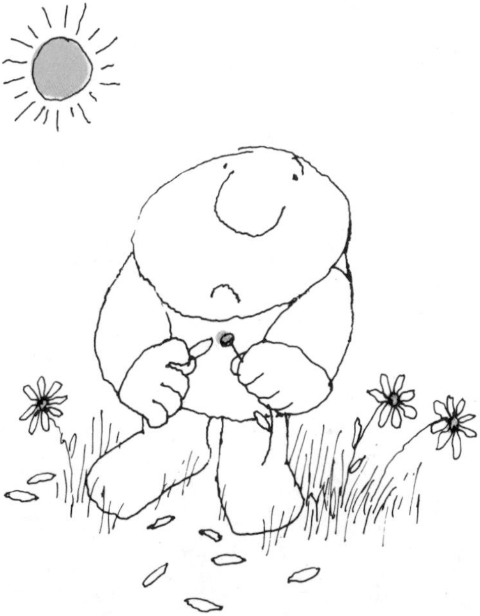

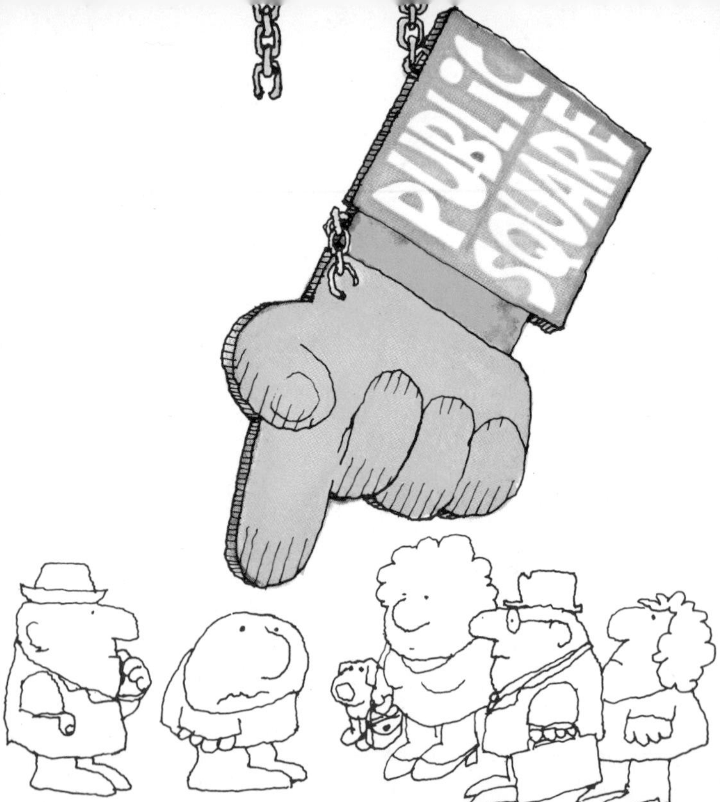
PUBLIC SQUARE

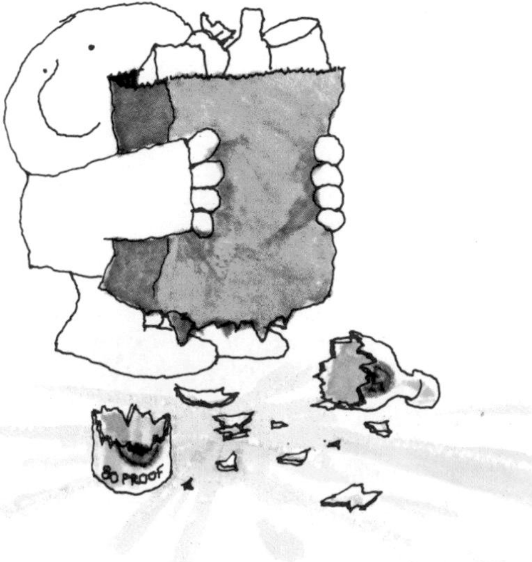
80 PROOF

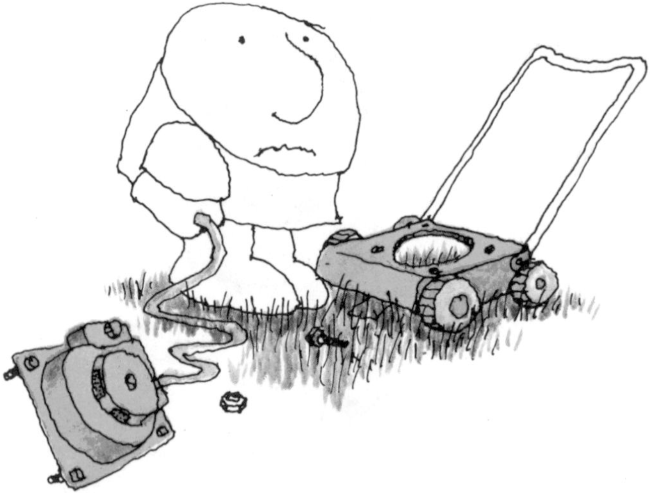

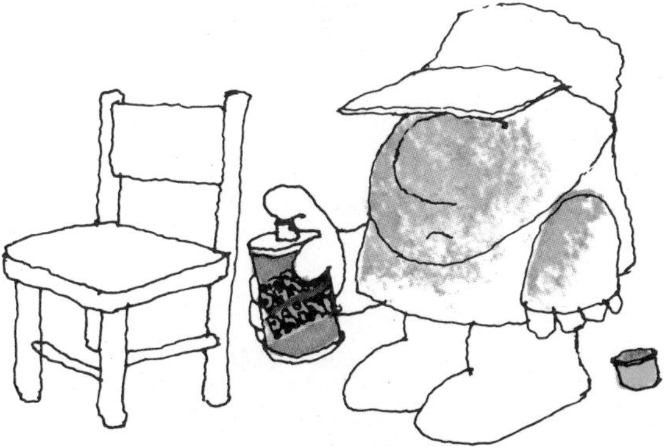

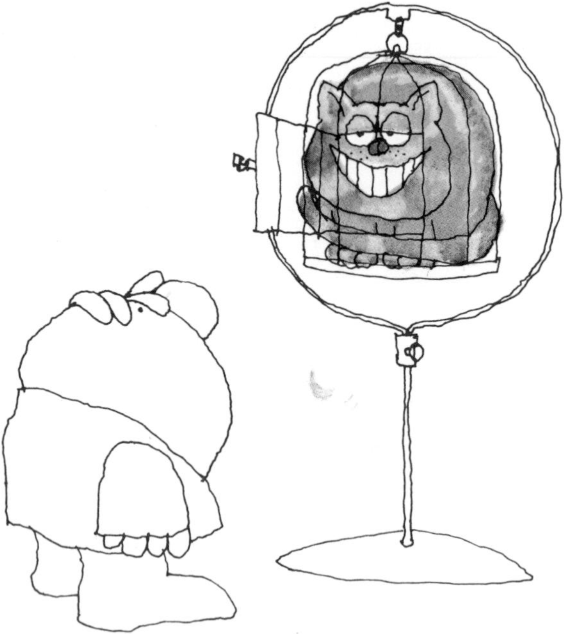

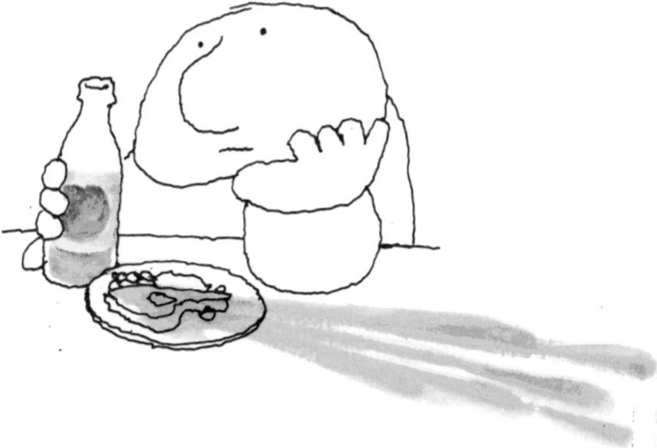

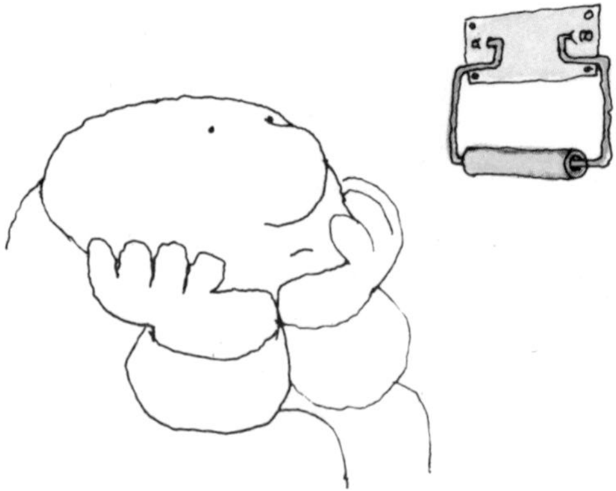

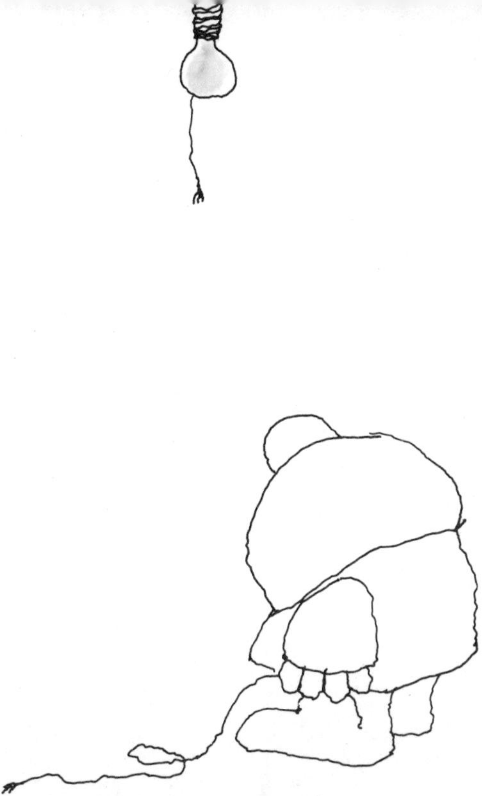

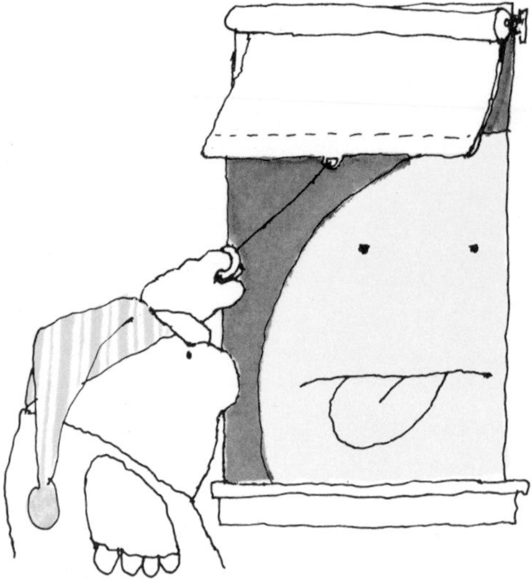